CONTENTS

CHAPTER IV : SWIMMING

I. GENERAL CONSIDERATIONS

Swimming is considered the most *complete* of all the exercises.

A complete exercise must at once be hygienic, aesthetic and functional; it must develop absolute strength per se as well as sustained strength and develop skill as well as mental energy.

Swimming fulfills all these conditions:

1) Its *hygienic effect* is intense: swimming activates all the major functions of the organism, particularly respiration; it also cleanses the skin and builds resilience to cold; finally, it is done outdoors. (Translator's comment: bear in mind that historically speaking, indoor pools were not in existence at the time of Hébert's authoring of the book).

2) Its action is very effective on the *amplification of the thorax* and *the increase in respiratory capacity*. Indeed, in all manners of swimming, the arms are constantly brought beyond the head in the alignment of the trunk, which produces an expansion of the ribs and results in a widening of the thoracic cage. Moreover, the disturbance produced by the body of water and the vigor of the muscular effort force to breathe long and deep.

3) It also has a very intense action on the *development of the entire musculature*, as it requires various muscular contractions of the arms, legs, trunk and head (neck muscles).

   Generally, all these contractions, being very expanded, constitute wonderful exercises for the stretching of the joints and limbs; they are also excellent for the straightening of the spinal column.

4) It requires, to go far and quickly, a *perfect coordination of movements* and an *adequate rhythm*.

5) Difficult exercises of diving or water rescue develop *dexterity*, *cold-blood* ("even keel"), *courage* and *self-confidence*.

6) Finally, all swimming exercises are of no-contest *usefulness*.

In order for a swim to be useful and effective, it is necessary to approach it in a specific manner.

One should not go in the water without knowing what to do ahead of time; otherwise, one risks a waste of time without possible progress.

To learn something, or simply to perfect one's technique, it is necessary to work methodically, to have a goal and outline a program.

The swim must be a true "lesson".

The swimming session, or "lesson", just like a training session, previously described, must be comprised of a certain amount of varied exercises, performed in a logical order, and must be perfectly regulated when it comes to energy expenditure.

A complete swimming lesson must contain:

1) One or several *sudden submersions* (of varying height), either head first, or feet first, then coming back to the surface.

2) A regular breast stroke swim, *on the stomach*, slowly, to begin. This manner of swimming is the best one to realign the spine and any hunching and help acquire or maintain good posture.

3) A swim *on the back*. Swimming on the back provides rest after a swim of a certain duration on the stomach; this stroke is also indispensable to be adept at during rescues.

4) An underwater *"dive"*, either starting from an elevation, or at surface level. This exercise consists in staying as long as possible underwater, the body fully submerged.

5) A period of complete rest, called *"floating"*. No arm or leg movement is to take place during this exercise.

6) One or more *"hauls"*, using the fastest swimming methods.

7) Finally, finish the lesson with a few slow strokes, on the stomach or the back, in order to restore enough calm in the breathing and circulation, before exiting the water.

Such is the "complete" program of a swim, both hygienic and functional.

Propulsion in the water results from a series of powerful impulses produced by an adequate movement from the upper and lower limbs.

It must be noted that all manners of progressing in the water are based on the same principle. The propulsion effort is produced by:

- The suddenness of the legs coming closer together, on one hand;
- The arm movements acting like a paddle or an oar, on the other hand.

The sudden closeness of the legs, which produces the greater powering effort, is comparable to the closing of the two blades of a pair of scissors. It can be done one of two ways:

- With the legs spread out, either laterally (e.g. ordinary breast stroke);
- Front to back, relative to the body (sagittal plane).

The movement of the arms can also be done one of two ways:

- Horizontally (e.g. breast stroke);
- Vertically (e.g. side stroke).

Finally, the movement of the legs, as that of the arms, can be alternated or simultaneous.

A swim can always be broken into four main phases:

1) *Starting position, or preparation*, of the limbs to produce effort;
2) *Effort*;
3) *Pause*, limbs extended in order to let the body flow and take advantage of the propulsion effort;
4) *Return* of the limbs to the starting position.

The work done by the limbs between two consecutive returns to the starting position constitute what is called a full "stroke", or *complete* movement.

The swimming *cadence* is the number of strokes, or complete movements executed in one minute.

Points of consideration:

- ◉ *Distance or resistance swims*, allowing to perform long swims with minimal fatigue;

- ◉ *Speed swims*, where one seeks maximal speed during short distance.

The *manner of breathing* in all styles is of capital importance.

The *inhale* takes place at the end of the pause, at the beginning of the return of the limbs to the starting position, when the body is slightly elevated. It is very quick and is usually done with an open mouth.

The *exhale* is done with the mouth closed. It is slow and lasts the entirety of the time not allocated for inhaling.

Respiration must be regulated according to the cadence of each stroke.

During distance swims, where the cadence is relatively slow, inhale at each complete stroke.

For speed swims, where the cadence is quicker, inhale only after one, two or three full strokes.

The economical cadence in distance swims is evidently that which matches a cadence of normal breathing, meaning 15 to 20 complete strokes per minute, on average.

Swimming exercises must have a dual goal: to each anyone to get themselves out of trouble under all circumstances, and to be of use to others by knowing how to rescue. They are made up of 3 categories:

1) The various ways to progress and maintain oneself at the surface of the water;

2) The "work" on and under water;

3) Rescue exercises.

II. CLASSIC ELEMENTARY SWIMMING STYLES

Swimming on the stomach or "breast stroke". – Back stroke. – Swimming upright. – "Floating".

I. BREAST STROKE.

The simplest and most natural way to maintain oneself on the surface of the water is to learn how to execute a breast stroke, or stroke while swimming on the stomach (prone).

Experience shows, indeed, that it is nearly impossible to get a novice to float without any movement or to be able to turn onto their back.

On the other hand, the breast stroke deserves special study, as it is the alphabet of swimming. The simplicity of its mechanics allows the obvious realization of the necessary efforts to progress in a body of water.

Once this style is well understood and executed correctly, all other methods of swimming can be learned rapidly.

The breast stroke comprises four principal phases:

1st Phase: *Starting position or preparation*

Figure 1. Breast stroke on the stomach: starting position or preparation.

Bend the legs by spreading the knees as much as possible, feet flexed and toes pointing out.

Place the elbows close to the body and bend the forearms so as to join the hands, palms facing down and horizontal, mid-chest level.

2nd Phase: *Impulse effort*

Extend the arms ahead of the body, palms still facing down. At once, extend the legs in the alignment of the thighs by pushing the water away with the sole of the feet, feet remaining flexed with the toes pointing out.

Figure 2. Breast stroke on the stomach: 1st part of impulse effort. Lateral extension of lower limbs, feet always flexed; arms extended beyond the head.

Bring the legs straight completely together, toes touching, with a full and complete extension of the feet.

Do not pause between the extension of the legs and the bringing of the legs together.

3rd Phase: *Pause, arms and legs extended*

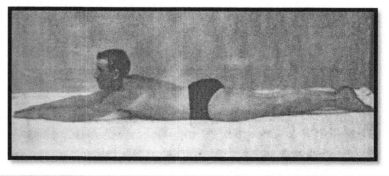

Figure 3. 2nd part of impulse effort: end of impulse after the "scissoring" of the legs, feet extended; also body position during the pause.

Mark a pause, legs and arms extended, in order to let the body glide and maximally benefit from the impulse effort provided by the extension and joining of the legs.

4th Phase: *Horizontal and lateral arm movement; deep inhale and return of the limbs to their starting position.*

Figure 4. Lateral and horizontal arm movement, palms out. Take a deep inhale during this movement.

Extend the arms and turn the palms to the outside as much as possible. Deeply inhale during the arm movement.

As soon as the arms are in line with the shoulders, bend them and return them to their initial position, keeping the palms flat.

Bend the legs at once and also return them to the starting position.

In this style of swimming, the forward propulsion of the body is due to the extension and the bringing back together of the legs as well as the lateral spreading of the arms.

The arm movement must begin at the moment the impulse from the body begins to decrease.

The swimmer, as ability and experience develops, learns to determine this moment quite accurately.

During the various phases of swimming: active period, preparation and pause, a proper rhythm is necessary.

The execution of the preparation movements ought not to counterbalance the effect of the active period movements.

It is interesting to observe, from this standpoint, novices who, despite considerable efforts deployed in order to move forward, remain in place.

In this case, there is an equal effort in the active as well as preparation movement periods.

The produced beneficial effect by the breast stroke movements depends on not only perfect coordination, but also on the breathing manner.

As the moment where the lateral spreading of the arms begins, the body is slightly elevated as a result of the impulse from the legs, which is never rendered in a perfectly horizontal plane.

The spreading of the arms has for effect the maintenance of the body sufficiently elevated to allow for the head to be fully emerged.

This is the moment where one must choose to deeply breathe in, considering that the speed of the body is relatively slower during this stroke's period, the head's drive back being weaker immediately after the leg action.

The impulse effort produced by the extension of the legs, pushing against the water with the sole of the flexed feet, is of relatively low consideration.

The most important effort is produced by the movement bringing the legs together.

This movement can be accurately compared to the closing of a pair of scissors. The value of the "scissoring" is increased by the extension of the feet, which begins immediately after the extension of the legs.

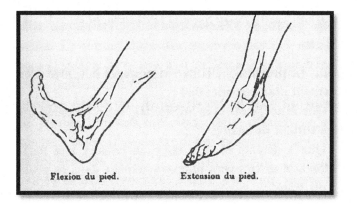

Figure 5. Foot flexion and foot extension, which have a great importance in the various swimming styles.

The movements that determine the propulsion (lateral spreading of the arms, extension and reunion of the legs) constitute the *active phase* of the breast stroke. They must be performed *energetically and vigorously*.

The other movements (forward arm extension and return of the arms and legs to the starting position) hinder progression, as they cause a slight recoil movement. They must therefore be executed without brusqueness and be relatively slow in relation to the active phase movements.

The duration of the pause, which follows the impulse, varies; it depends essentially on the value of the impulse effort given by the legs.

Breathing in happens quickly, in one "inhale" with the open mouth.

The exhale is slow, mouth closed, for the remainder of the stroke's duration.

The head can remain in constant extension and above the water. However, this constant forced extension becomes quickly tiring.

It is preferable, for a longer course, to extend the head only for inhales and to match this extension with the lateral spreading of the arms. The rest of the time, the head is slightly dropped or submerged.

The propulsion, and consequently the speed reached, is that much more considerable factoring that:

1) The body is horizontal, without having the legs stick out of the water;

2) Thee extension and the "scissoring" occur in one direction in alignment with the trunk;

3) Coordination is "most" perfect;

4) Movements have more extension and the cadence is more regular;

If the body is too inclined on the horizontal, a portion of the legs impulse only serves to elevate the body out of the water rather than propel it forward. The body progresses in bounds rather than glides.

The same phenomenon occurs when the effort from the legs is not given in a plane aligned with the trunk.

This is why it is necessary to throw the knees as laterally as possible, or, if desired, to only bend the thighs laterally and not forward.

The spreading of the legs or knees isn't necessarily as wide as possible, it depends on the energy of the "scissoring". It's just like running or walking, where the stride length varies according to individuals and the type of course covered.

To learn the breast stroke, the best way to proceed is the following:

◉ Learn how to correctly do the moves on dry land.

◉ Go in the water, waist or chest deep. Exercise the leg movements while holding on to something with the hands; then stand upright and perform the arm movements.

◉ Only attempt the stroke when the leg movements feel natural. This last condition is indispensable. The combination of movements of the upper and lower limbs will be easily performed once the leg movements are correct.

The first mistake from beginners is to always do an incorrect leg movement, resulting from a lack of dry land practice or too few trials in the water holding on to something.

Other mistakes consist of doing the movements at high speed; of not extending enough in the water, and of breathing randomly, which can cause suffocation or absorption of big gulps of liquid.

II. BACK STROKE

Once the mechanics of the performance of the breast stroke have been well understood and perfectly executed, the learning of the back stroke is quick and easy.

The movement of the lower limbs is, indeed, for this style, identical to that of the breast stroke.

As for the movement of the arms, it is extremely simple.

The back stroke, like the breast stroke, comprises 4 main phases:

1st Phase: *Starting position or preparation.* [INSERT PIC]

Bend the legs the same way as the breast stroke, meaning with the knees spread out as widely as possible and the feet flexed and turned outward.

Bend the forearms at once, elbows to body, palms flat at the middle of the chest, fingertips touching.

2nd Phase: *Impulse effort.*

Extend the legs in the alignment of the thighs, by pushing the water off with the sole of the feet still flat.

[ORIGINAL TEXT MISSING, PHOTOS BLURRY.

SPECULATIVE TEXT:

Extend the arms over the head in line with the trunk, palms facing out, then bring the straight arms laterally towards the side of the body, palms facing towards the body and the direction of the arm movement, at the same time as the legs perform the "scissoring" action of closing together]

Pause, the legs extended in the alignment of the trunk, feet together and extended, arms straight alongside the body, hands flat on the side of the thighs. Let the body glide in this position.

4th Phase: *Deep inhale and return to starting position.*

The impulse effort has for effect to lift the body up slightly and make the head emerge. Take advantage of that moment to take a deep and fast inhale. As soon as the impulse given to the body ceases, bring the lower limbs back to their starting position.

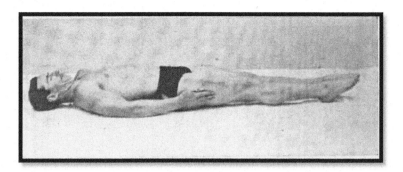

Figure 6. End of impulse effort on the back stroke, after the leg scissoring and the arrival of the arms alongside the body. The body stays so during the pause.

In the backstroke, the forward propulsion of the body is due to the extension and bringing together back of the legs, as well as the lateral movement of the arms.

These two movements, instead of being alternated like in the prone breaststroke, are simultaneous, the effort of the arms coinciding exactly with the effort of the legs.

Figure 7. Back stroke: end of impulse effort: head and upper body emerge. Take advantage of this moment to take a long, deep inhale.

All the remarks made in relation to the leg movements for the breaststroke (extension and reunion of the legs, foot position) are also applicable to the backstroke; no further explanation is necessary.

The extension movement of the legs, as well as that of the "closing" or "scissoring" in the lateral direction are much easier to execute correctly on the back than on the stomach.

Also, the spreading out of the knees is more natural and is done effortlessly.

The movement of the arms is also less strenuous, the shoulders having no effort to produce during the pause.

The head is continuously kept in the alignment of the trunk, or slightly bend towards the chest; there is no effort to extend the neck. In general, beginners keep the head bent to avoid letting the water fully cover it after each impulse effort.

For all these reasons, the backstroke is far less tiring than the breast stroke.

It is a bit slower than the latter. The effort of the arms and legs being simultaneous, instead of being alternated, there is a resulting considerable recoil, as well as a sinking of the body upon return of the limbs to the starting position.

In the breast stroke, this sinking is very small, since the body is supported till the last moment of the preparation by the horizontal motion of the arms.

The manner of breathing is more important and slightly harder during the backstroke than the breaststroke. Indeed, the head is almost fully covered by water during the preparation and the action of the limbs. It emerges naturally at the end of the impulse as a result of the body's position, which is never perfectly horizontal at the moment of effort of the limbs.

The inhale is taken at the end of the pause, immediately before the return of the limbs to their starting position. It is quick and deep and is done in one "intake", the mouth open.

The exhale takes place with the mouth closed, for the entire duration of a single stroke.

There is another, far more effective manner to perform the arm movements:

- In the starting position, the arms are placed above the head in the alignment of the trunk, palms out and vertical. During the impulse effort, the arms are brought completely extended alongside the body, palms vertical.

- The return of the arms to the starting position is done by raising the arms vertically in front of the body, parallel to one another, until they are placed above the head.

To learn to swim on the back, the most practical way is the following: standing chest high in the water, let yourself slowly fall backwards and simply do the leg movements, maintaining the arms alongside the body, palms facing down and horizontal. Once a bit of confidence has built up, spread the arms laterally a little palms facing down, and bring them back to the body by turning the palms vertically.

Gradually increase the amplitude of the arm movements until their full range of motion as the leg movements become more natural.

Common mistakes made by beginners are similar than in the breast stroke: rushed movements without pause, incomplete extension, folding of the body in half, head above water for the duration of each stroke, random breathing.

III. UPRIGHT (STANDING) SWIMMING.

Swimming upright consists of being perpendicular to the surface of the water. In this position, one can stay in place, go forward, backwards, laterally or spin around.

This manner of swimming is very useful when one wishes to:

- Observe what goes on around oneself;

- Drift with the current;

- Await rescue;

- Tread water while heavily attired;

- Undress in the water;

- Hold a heavy object or carry an object without getting it wet;

- Hold a tired person, etc., etc.

Upright swimming is made up of four principal phases like the previously described styles.

The lower limbs perform the ordinary leg movements of the breast and back strokes. As for the upper limbs' movements, they vary according to whether one wants to stay in place, go forward or backwards.

In order to stay in place in the vertical position, the following movements need to be performed:

1st Phase: *Starting position or preparation.*

Bend the arms, elbows at the body, palms flat at mid chest level, alms facing down and horizontal, fingertips touching.

Bend the lower limbs, knees spread out laterally, feet flexed and turned out.

2nd Phase: *Impulse effort.*

Extend the arms horizontally and lower them, straightened, towards the thighs, palms still down and horizontal.

Extend the legs laterally, feet flexed then bring them together by extending the feet.

3rd Phase: *Pause.*

Keep the arms extended and straight, palms down and vertical.

Keep the legs straight and together.

4th Phase: *Deep inhale and return of the limbs to their starting position.*

At the end of the impulse, the body finding itself elevated vertically takes a deep breath in at that moment.

Raise the arms in front of the body by turning the palms vertically, then return to the starting position by putting the palms back to horizontal. Bend the legs and also position them back into the starting position.

Based on this description, if one wants to remain in place in the upright swim, the movement of the arms, instead of taking place horizontally, like in the previous styles, is executed vertically.

The impulse effort of the upper and lower limbs takes place simultaneously like in the back stroke.

In order to move forward, backwards or laterally in this upright position, the movement of the lower limbs doesn't change, but, depending on the chosen direction, the arms are used differently.

To move forward, the movement of the upper limbs is the following:

1st Phase: *Starting position or preparation.*

No change.

2nd Phase: *Impulse effort.*

Extend the arms ahead of the body, palms horizontal. Turn the palms vertically facing the body, bending the wrists, fingertips joined.

Bring then the hands in contact with the chest, palms still vertical.

3rd Phase: *Pause.*

Keep the hands flat on the chest.

4th Phase: *Return to the starting position.*

Simply place the hands horizontally.

To move backwards:

1st Phase: *Starting position or preparation.*

No change.

2nd Phase: *Impulse effort.*

Extend the arms ahead of the body and turn the palms outward as far as possible, thumbs pointing down, fingertips joined.

3rd Phase: *Pause.*

Keep the arms extended, palms facing out.

4th Phase: *Return to the starting position.*

Place the palms horizontally, then bring the hands to the chest.

To move laterally (to the right, for example):

1st Phase: *Starting position.*

Right arm extended laterally, palm flat. Left arm in its normal position.

2nd Phase: *Impulse effort.*

Right arm movement: Turn the palm vertically and bring it flat against the chest.

Left arm movement: Extend the left arm to the left, palm turned outward as far as possible, thumb under.

3rd Phase: *Pause.*

Right hand flat against the chest. Left arm extended, palm facing out.

4th Phase: *Return to the starting position.*

Place the right hand flat and extend the right arm laterally. Turn the left hand flat and bring it to the chest.

To make forward, backwards or lateral movement easier, it is necessary to slightly lean the upper body in the desired direction.

To move laterally, one of the two arms can be used, the other holding its initial position throughout, with the palm flat.

The progress of the body results solely from the action of the hands, which, taking support against the liquid mass, bring the body closer to them in forward progress, push it away in backwards progress, or bring it closer on one side while pushing away the other side in lateral progress.

The position of the hands thus is of great importance.

In all movements of preparation or return to starting position, the hands, having then no particular task to accomplish, must oppose the least amount of resistance possible. The opposite takes place during the impulse effort.

For instance, in order to remain vertical, the initial return to the starting position is done with the hands vertical. The hands turned horizontally would have a sinking effect on the body.

In the forward progression movement, the hands are thrown horizontally forward; the palms, held vertically, would have a pushing-back effect on the body.

In order to completely turn in place, to the right for example, begin by bringing the head to the right and by moving the left shoulder and hip. Then, do the arm movement as for the lateral progression, by making sure to put the right arm as far back as possible behind the shoulder line, and the left arm slightly ahead of the body.

Do the opposite motions to turn left.

The learning of the upright swimming style is simple and easy.

On needs, from swimming on the stomach, to reduce gradually the incline of the body until it is in a vertical position.

The head remains upright or slightly angled backwards.

Breathing takes place easily, the impulse effort of the lower limbs having tendency to bring the body upwards.

IV. "FLOATING".

To "float" consists of staying immobile in the water, in a position of equilibrium, motionless.

This manner of remaining at the surface of the water is of non-contest utility in the following circumstances:

- ◉ To rest in case of fatigue;

- ◉ To await rescue;

- ◉ In case of cramping;

- ◉ When the limbs are encumbered with any object: ropes, clothing, weeds, etc.;

- ◉ To get over whirlpools, etc.

The simplest manner to manage "floating" is by successively executing the series of movements, which will be further indicated.

Begin by swimming upright by staying in place as previously explained.

In this position, cease the lower limb action by keeping the legs straight and joined together, the feet hanging naturally.

Gradually reduce the amplitude of the upper limbs until their action is that of a simple sculling movement of the hands.

This sculling movement is performed with the arms along the body, wrists straight, hands in extension acting as flippers and cutting the water with lateral figure 8-shaped movements.

Gradually cease sculling. Leave the hands stiff, palms horizontal and flat. The arms can remain along the body or extended laterally.

Once all effort from the limbs has ceased, the body finds itself to be like a buoy abandoned at the surface of the water. It first sinks, then resurfaces and so on until equilibrium is reached.

Being submitted to no vertical impulse, it resurfaces less and less after each oscillation.

In order for breathing to remain possible, the head must be slightly thrown back and the chin must be lifted in order for the nose and the mouth to be emerged.

It is necessary than the reduction, then cessation of the limb movements take place slowly and gradually in order to maximally reduce the vertical oscillations of the body.

The equilibrium position is never perfect, the body always oscillates slightly vertically.

Outside of the motion of the water and of the involuntary contractions of the muscles, the breathing movements only suffice to produce these oscillations as a result of the changes Figure 8. Body position while floating: palms horizontal, paralle to the surface, same with the feet, head thrown back so that the nose and mouth emerge.in volume of the body. Immediately after each inhale, the body tends to rise; during the exhale, it sinks slightly. It is always at the moment of the rise that one must inhale quickly and deeply.

Figure 9. Balanced and floating position: the body oscillates vertically. The floating line is above the axis of the ears.

23

Breathing must be regulated in perfect accord with the oscillations.

Learning to float can start from swimming on the back. Just proceed as previously described starting from the upright swimming style.

Stop the leg movements, then gradually reduce the arm movements until completely reducing their action to a sculling motion with the hands.

Leave the hands flat, arms along the body or spread out laterally.

When floating, the equilibrium position of the body takes place according to an angle, which depends on the floatability of the individual.

This angle/incline varies from the vertical to the horizontal position. It can be assumed with the upper body falling backwards or forward, both positions being symmetrical. The most natural and most practical, because of the head's position, is evidently the backwards incline.

The "line of floatation" varies among individuals by 3cm or 4cm (1.2" to 1.6") below the earhole to about 2cm (0.8") above.

People with great floatability, meaning those whose floatation line is well under the axis of the ears, have no need to throw their head back, or to keep the palms flat and horizontal. They float without effort and breathe with great ease.

On the contrary, subjects whose line of floatation is above the axis of the ears must throw the head back in order to let the nose and mouth emerge. From time to time, to inhale more easily, they must assist their body in rising with a slight pressure movement of the hands or extension of the feet.

The incline of the body in equilibrium can be modified by proper displacements of certain parts.

Floating horizontally, or "doing the plank" and floating vertically constitute two separate cases.

In general, those with greater floatability float without difficulty in these two positions, the arms along the body or extended laterally.

Others must modify their equilibrium as follows:

- To remain vertical, bring the arms ahead of the body or extend the legs backwards.

- To remain horizontal, extend the arms behind the head as far as necessary.

III. VARIOUS SWIMMING STYLES FOR ENDURANCE AND SPEED.

Outside simple styles like the breast stroke or swimming on the back, as well as upright swimming, which, notwithstanding, suffice in all circumstances to cope or even perform difficult rescues, other particularly useful styles exist when one seeks to:

- ◉ Cover a long distance;

- ◉ Proceed quickly to a specific spot;

- ◉ Cover a few meters at maximal speed.

These styles are in themselves only derived or lightly modified from the ordinary prone breast stroke.

Their mechanics of progressing is analogous to that of basic swim styles: stomach or back swimming, meaning they contain all or part of the 4 main phases of those styles: preparation, impulse effort, pause and return to starting position.

All the comments previously made relative to the various phases and their rhythm of execution, the importance of the closing or "scissoring" of the legs, the breathing etc., are all applicable. It is therefore not necessary to recall those in detail every time.

It is important to distinguish:

1) *Endurance or distance swims*, both less tiring and faster than ordinary breast stroke on the stomach, and also more practical to cover long distances;

2) *Speed swims*, allowing to reach maximal speed, but not sustainable for long because of the great energetic expenditure they require.

From a functional standpoint, it is not necessary to know and practice all endurance or speed swimming styles.

It is necessary to choose, among the speed or endurance swims, the manners that apply to the most to personal aptitude, which at once provide the best practical results.

Some styles require, in order to be performed correctly, a relatively great ease of movement, and a long practice is required before their use can provide satisfactory results.

V. ENDURANCE OR DISTANCE SWIMS.

Side stroke.- Ordinary Indian breast stroke. – Non-stop Indian breast stroke.

Endurance swims are executed with the body entirely laying on the right or left side in a much less tiring position than the regular breast stroke on the stomach. The latter is sustained for a finite amount of time, as it tires the low back, neck and shoulders, since it requires a nearly constant effort from these three body parts.

In side swimming, there is no extension effort in either the neck, or the back, and the muscles that raise the arms only work in intervals instead of working in a nearly non-stop fashion.

Moreover, the body offers less resistance in liquid mass when placed on its side than on the stomach; it cuts through the water better.

The various ways to side swim are executed:

1) By utilizing the regular breast stroke movement of the legs;

2) By performing the opening and closing movements of the legs in a *front to back of the body direction*. The latter is more natural than the former, given the position of the body.

In all cases the arm movements are done the same way.

The descriptions that follow are done assuming the body is laying on its right side.

Swimming on the left side is evidently executed according to the same principles.

From an educational standpoint, it is evident that side swims but be performed equally well on the right as well as left sides.

1st Style: side stroke

Figure 10. Side stroke: starting position for impulse effort. Left: upper arm underwater. Right: upper arm above water.

1st Phase: Starting position or preparation.

Slightly bend the arms, elbows close to the body.

Place the left hand under the chin at right shoulder level, the right hand ahead of the right shoulder, palms under, fingers extended and together in the same direction as the alignment of the body.

Bend the lower limbs by spreading the knees as widely as possible, feet flexed and toes pointing out (like in the breast stroke on the stomach).

2nd Phase: Impulse effort.

Figure 11. Left: 1st part of impulse: lateral extension of the legs prior to their returning to alignment with the body; forward extension of the right arm, pull with left. Right: end of impulse and position of the body during the pause.

Extend the right arm fully forward and horizontally, in the alignment of the body, palm down.

At the same time, pull the left arm horizontally backwards alongside the body, by pushing off the water with a slightly and tightly cupped hand, the elbow coming out of the water.

Bring the legs close together completely, toes together by extending the feet with full force (just like in the breast stroke on the stomach).

3rd Phase: Pause, arms and legs extended.

Mark a pause, legs and arms extended, in order to let the body glide and benefit as much as possible of the impulse just given by the extension and bringing together of the legs, as well as the effort produced by the left arm pulled backwards.

4th Phase: Return to the starting position.

Lower the straight right arm in a vertical plane until it touches the right thigh, hand slightly closed and cupped; bend the arm then pull it back to the starting position by bringing it alongside and close to the body, palm first vertical, then turned face up and finally facing down.

Bring the left arm to the starting position by bringing it underwater close to the body, fingers extended and joined together.

At the same time, bend the lower limbs and also bring them back to their starting position (like in the breast stroke on the stomach).

Inhale at the end of the impulse, during the return of the limbs to the starting position, while the upper body is lifted as a result of the right arm's effort.

Exhale the rest of the time.

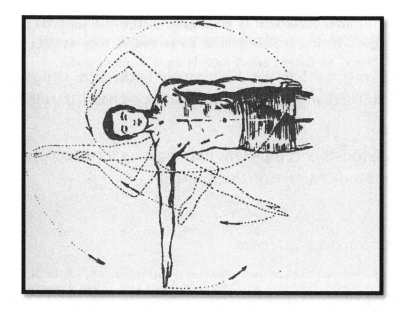

Figure 12. Side stroke: detailed arm movement. Body assumed on the right side with the upper arm working above the water surface. During the return motion of the upper arm in attack position above the head, be mindful of always projecting the shoulder as forward as possible at the same time as the arm.

Keep the head in the line of the trunk and avoid leaning towards the upper shoulder (common novice mistake to avoid getting the face covered by water at each new impulse effort). Slightly turn it to the left to inhale.

There is a second way to execute the movement of the upper arm (or left). Instead of working under the surface of the water, work the upper arm *over* in the following fashion.

1st Phase: Starting position.

Left arm above water, slightly bent, elbow elevated.

Left hand slightly ahead of the head just above the surface of the water, fingers cupped.

2nd Phase: Impulse effort.

Only enter the left hand in the water to the wrist. Pull the left arm back, along and close to the body, with producing effort with the cupped hand.

3rd Phase: Pause.

Let the left arm extend under water alongside the body, palm turned up.

4th Phase: Return to the starting position.

Pull the left arm from the water vertically, bend it and throw it beyond the head while bringing at the same time the left shoulder strongly forward. Position the left hand as described in the 1st phase.

The return motion of the left arm above the water presents the advantage of *not impairing speed*, but it is more tiring to execute than the return motion from under.

2nd Style: Indian stroke.

The arm movements are identical to those of the side stroke.

1st Phase: Starting position.

Figure 13. The Indian Stroke: Starting position for impulse effort. Left: with upper arm under water. Right: upper arm above water.

Arm position: left hand underwater ahead of the right shoulder or above water slightly in front of the head. Right hand underwater in front of the head (like for the side stroke).

Leg position: spread the legs out the following way: throw the left or upper leg slightly ahead of the line of the body at a 45° angle approximately, either slightly bent, or completely straight, foot flexed, meaning the toes pointing towards the shin.

Bend the right or lower leg as much as possible, the heel close to the right thigh, foot extended, keeping the thigh in line with the trunk as much as possible, without throwing the knee forward or backwards.

2nd Phase: Impulse effort.

Arm movements: extend the right arm forward and horizontally and at the same time pull the left arm backwards (like for the side stroke).

Leg movements:

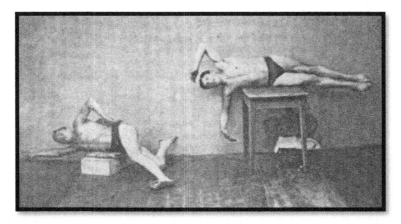

Figure 14. 1st : Left: end of impulse and body position during pause. The movement of closing or scissoring of the legs in a front to back direction is over; the right arm is extended forward, palm down, the left arm is pulled backwards touching the left thigh. 2nd: Right: work of the right arm (lower arm) and at the same time return of legs to starting position.

Bring the legs in line with the body by executing a vigorous scissoring closing movement with the legs in a front to back direction. Completely extend the left foot as the left leg is brought backwards.

Extend the lower limbs, knees and feet joined, toes also extended.

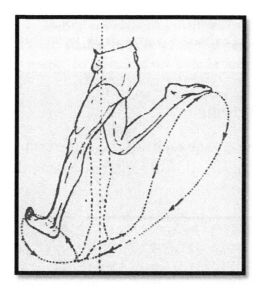

Figure 15.Detailed movement of the legs, assuming body leaning on right side. The spreading of the legs happens in a front to back direction, not laterally. The highs remain in contact. The left foot of the upper leg is flexed, the lower leg's foot is extended at the start of the "scissor action". The effort from the upper leg is done with the hamstring, while that of the lower legs is done with the quadriceps.

3rd Phase: Pause.

Mark a pause, lower legs joined and straight, left arm against the body, right arm extended horizontally and forward (like in the side stroke).

4th Phase: Return to the starting position.

Arm movements: lower the right arm vertically, bring it close to the body, then back to the starting position. Execute the return of the left arm either from under or over the surface of the water (like in the side stroke).

Leg movements: Spread out the legs, the left or upper leg forward and the right or lower leg backwards as described in the 1st phase.

Like in the side stroke: inhale at the end of the impulse effort during the return of the lower limbs to their starting position, when the movement of the right arm raises the upper body. Exhale during the rest of the time.

Keep the head in line with the body without leaning it towards the left or upper shoulder. Turn it slightly to the left to take a breath in.

3rd Style: non-stop Indian stroke.

This swimming style is composed exactly of the same arm and leg movements as the standard Indian stroke. The association of various movements in relation to one another is the only differentiator.

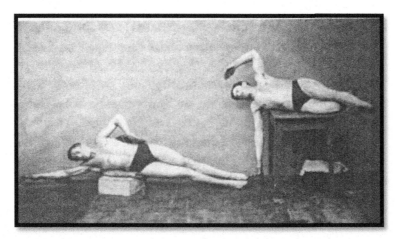

Figure 16. Left: 1st impulse effort; pulling of the left arm backwards, extension of the right arm forward, spreading of the legs. Left: 2nd impulse effort: closing of the legs, return of the left arm forward, lowering of the right arm and return to starting position.

There is no pause. While one set of limbs returns to its starting position, the other set of limbs executes the work necessary for progressing.

Fatigue is greater than in the standard Indian stroke, but its output is superior. The body, always under a constant impulse effort, progresses in the water in a continuous manner, instead of moving forward through successive pushes. The association of movements from the standard Indian stroke making up the non-stop Indian stroke is the following:

1st Phase: Starting position.

Arm position (no change): right hand ahead of the right shoulder, left hand under or above water.

Leg position: legs extended and together, feet extended (like in the 3rd phase of the standard Indian stroke).

2nd Phase: 1st Impulse effort.

Arm movements (no change): Extend the right arm forward and pull the left arm backwards.

Leg movements: spread the legs out: left or upper leg forward, right or lower leg backwards like in the 1st phase of the standard Indian stroke.

3rd Phase: 2nd Impulse effort.

Arm movements: return the left arm forward to the starting position. Lower the right arm and return it to the starting position as well (like in the 4th phase of the standard Indian stroke).

Leg movements: closing or scissoring of the legs (like in the 2nd phase of the standard Indian stroke).

At the end of this 2nd impulse effort, the limbs are in position to repeat the 1st effort. No pause should break up these two efforts.

The swim is thus reduced to a series of successive and non-stop/ongoing executions of the 2nd and 3rd phases.

NOTE: The movement of the legs in the standard Indian stroke or in the non-stop Indian stroke can also be made more effective by executing it with one of the following two manners:

(Do not try to swim using one of these two methods prior to possessing perfected mechanics of the standard way).

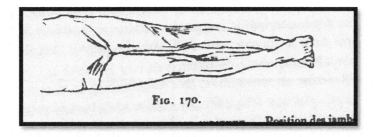

Fig. 170.

Position des jamb

Figure 17. Leg crossing: foot and leg position at the end of the impulse effort and during the pause.

1) Perform the leg closing or "scissoring" by crossing the feet.

Instead of bringing the legs together and of extending them at the moment of closing them, crisscross them in the following fashion: turn the toes inward so as to place the sole of the right foot on the left foot's instep. Return to the starting position by uncrossing the feet.

By proceeding in this fashion, the water is better taken and cut through during the return of the legs to their starting position than in the standard movement. Any work detrimental to propulsion is thus alleviated.

2) Perform a "double scissor kick".

Instead of keep the legs together and straight upon closing of the legs, continue spreading the straight legs; the right leg going forward, the left leg backwards, feet extended. Keep the legs in this position during the pause in the standard Indian stroke.

By this process of crossing of the legs, an additional scissoring action occurs at the moment the legs return to their starting position, very favorable to propulsion.

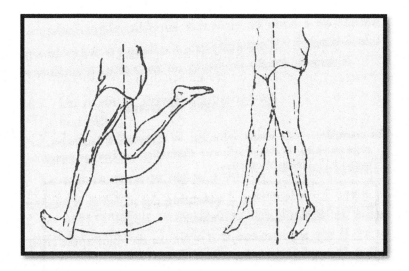

Figure 18. Double scissor: Left: starting position of the legs, body leaning right. Right: starting position at end of impulse effort and during pause, Legs open, upper leg behind lower leg.

VI. SPEED SWIMS.

The "mariner". –Standard cut. – Indian cut. –Doggy paddle or standard alternated cut. –Crawling swim or alternating Indian cut.

The mechanics of execution of the speed swims presents the following particulars:

1) There are no pauses or rests after each impulse effort, opposite of what took place in the endurance, or distance swims. While one set of limbs executes the active part of a movement, the other set of limbs performs its return to the starting position. The swim is thus made up of a series of impulse efforts alternatively produced by each set of limbs.

2) The return to the starting position of the limbs is executed so as to *hinder propulsion as little as possible*. The return by the arms always takes place above water. Only the legs' return constitutes a hindrance in the work.

   In the crawling style, the movement of the legs can however be done in such a way so as to not hinder the propulsion at any moment.

3) *The arms have a very important role* from a body propulsion standpoint.

   In endurance swimming, the arms' effect on propulsion is of low consideration relative to that of the legs. It is logical, given that the upper limbs fatigue faster than the lower limbs. In speed swimming, on the contrary, the speed of progression is obtained by additional energetic efforts of the upper limbs.

4) The cadence of movements is faster than that of endurance swimming. Breathing doesn't occur at each impulse effort, but only after two or more successive efforts.

Speed swimming comprises:

1) The mariner style;

2) The standard cut;

3) The Indian cut;

4) The doggy paddle or standard cut with alternated leg movements;

5) The crawl, or crawling swim, also known as Indian cut with alternated leg movements.

Given the importance of the arm movements in speed swimming, specifically work their mechanics of execution by swimming without the use of the legs. Train to reach faster speeds only using the arms, legs remaining straight and closed together.

1st Style: The Mariner

Figure 19. Left: starting position for impulse effort. Right: end of impulse. The movement of lateral extension and leg closing is finished; left arm continues its circular horizontal motion, the palm of the hand is outward.

The mariner is done by using the movement of the legs of the standard breast stroke on the stomach. The movement with the arms is alternated.

Their effective work is identical to the one performed in the standard breast stroke on the stomach.

The body remains constantly on the stomach or slightly rolls to the right during the right arm's work, or left during the left arm's work.

1st Phase: starting position, or preparation.

Arms position: right arm extended alongside the body, right hand's touching the thigh with the palm facing up; left arm above water close to the surface, completely extended ahead of the head, hand palm facing down and in the line of the body, fingers extended and joined together.

Legs position: Legs are bent laterally, knees apart just like in the standard breast stroke on the stomach.

2nd Phase: impulse effort.

Extend and bring the legs back together vigorously as described in the standard breast stroke on the stomach.

Enter the left arm in the water, bring it horizontal and backwards to touch the left thigh, by keeping it extended and turning the palm outward in order to push off the water.

Maintain the right arm at the body.

3rd Phase: return to the starting position.

As the left arm arrives alongside the body, exit the right arm from the water and throw it to the starting position the left arm was in using one of two ways:

- ◉ Either vertically by bending it, then extending it above and beyond the head;

- ◉ Or horizontally by keeping it extended and performing a circular motion around the shoulder.

At the same time that the right arm is returning to the initial position, bend the legs laterally, knees apart, as described in the standard breast stroke on the stomach.

No pause separates the 2nd from the 3rd phase.

At the end of the 2nd phase, the limbs are in position to resume a new impulse effort, this time with action from the right arm instead of the left arm.

Inhale at the end of this impulse effort, at the precise moment when the chest rises as a result of the action of the arm pushing backwards. Exhale the rest of the time.

2nd Style: the standard cut.

Figure 20. Standard cut. Left: starting position for impulse effort. Right: 2nd part of impulse effort. In the first part of the effort, the lateral extension movement and closing of the legs is over. The left arm just completed a sculling motion from left to right with the left hand level with the right nipple. The left hand continues its effort on the water and touches the left upper thigh; at the same time the right arm gets out of the water and gets positioned beyond the head back in the starting position.

In the standard cut, the movement of the legs is the same as the one performed in the standard breast stroke on the stomach.

The body remains continuously horizontal, flat on the stomach, or slightly rolls to the right during the right arm's work, or left during the left arm's work.

1st Phase: starting position, or preparation.

Arms position: right arm extended along the body; right hand touches the right thigh, palm up.

Left arm above the water, slightly bent, elbow lifted high, left head slightly ahead of the head and close to the surface of the water, fingers bent forming a cup.

Legs position: Legs bent and knees spread apart (like in the in the standard breast stroke on the stomach).

2nd Phase: impulse effort and return of the limbs to their starting position.

Extend and unite the legs vigorously as in the in the standard breast stroke on the stomach.

Enter the left arm in the water. Do a sculling motion to the left, then the right with the right hand in order to move it forward and close to the chest level with the right nipple.

Throw it then so it touches the left thigh, palm facing up, left arm completely extended, in a position similar to that of the right arm in its starting position.

At the moment when the left hand is level with the right nipple, and while it performs the second part of its impulse effort, exit the right arm off the water and bring it above the head by *projecting the right shoulder forward as strongly as possible*. Keep the right arm slightly bent, elbow lifted high, and place the right hand slightly ahead of the head, just like the left hand was in its starting position, meaning close to the surface and fingers joined and cupped.

At the same time as the right arm is returning to its "attack" position, bend the legs, knees spread apart like in the standard breast stroke on the stomach.

At the end of this 2nd phase, the body is ready to resume a new impulse effort, this time with action from the right arm instead of the left arm.

Note that the 2nd phase is divided into two distinct parts:

- ◉ The first part comprises the extension of the lower limbs and approximately half of the left arm's work.

- ◉ The second part comprises the second part of the left arm's work and the return of the legs to their starting position.

The lower limbs only remain completely extended for a relatively short time.

One must not wait, like in the Mariner style, until one arm accomplishes its effective task and is returned alongside the body in order for the other arm to perform its return, as well as the legs' return to the starting position.

Inhale during the second part of the impulse effort, meaning during the return of an arm to its initial position, when the chest rises as a result of the effort produced by the other arm.

3rd Style: the Indian cut.

In the Indian cut, the active portion of the arms movement is executed in one of the following two ways:

1) Like the standard cut, meaning with a sculling action of the hand;

2) As described with the upper arm movement (working above water) of the Indian stroke, meaning directly bringing the hand from front to back.

The return of the arms to their starting position always takes place above water, like in the standard cut.

The movement of the legs is that of the standard breast stroke, meaning the opening and closing of the legs take place in a front to back direction in relation to the body.

In other words, the Indian cut is nothing more than an Indian stroke performed by getting the lower arm out of the water the same way as the upper arm.

Figure 21. Left: starting position for the 1st impulse. Right: 1st effort. The closing movement of the legs is completed; the left arm ends its effort and the right arm is positioned beyond the head, ready for the 2nd effort. In this style, there is only one leg movement for every 2 arm movements. During the return to start phase of the arms for the starting position, pay attention to always project the shoulder as far forward as possible, at the same time as the arm.

The body, instead of remaining continuously on the side like in the Indian stroke, rolls to the stomach for the lower arms exit out of the water. The body rolls back to the side during the working phase of the upper arm.

1ˢᵗ Phase: Starting position or preparation.

The body is sideways like in the Indian stroke.

Arms position: right arm stuck to the body and left arm above water like in the standard cut.

Legs position: Legs spread apart: left leg forward, right leg bent backwards like the Indian stroke on the right side.

2ⁿᵈ Phase: 1ˢᵗ impulse effort.

Bring the left arm close to the body by sculling with the hand like in the standard cut, or bring it directly by strongly pulling close in the water without sculling, like in the upper arm's movement in the Indian stroke.

Execute at the same time the closing or "scissoring" action of the legs, like in the Indian stroke.

As soon as the left arm starts its movement, turn the body on the stomach, get the right arm out of the water and bring it above the head in the starting position like the left arm was.

Keep the legs together and straight.

3ʳᵈ Phase: 2ⁿᵈ impulse effort.

Bring the right arm back by strongly pulling the water to you using one of the two ways mentioned for the left arm.

At the same time, return the body to the right side, get the left arm out of the water and bring it back to its starting position. Spread the legs and bring them back to the starting position.

At the end of the 3ʳᵈ phase, the limbs are in position to restart the 1ˢᵗ impulse effort.

Inhale during the 2ⁿᵈ impulse effort, when the left arm returns to the starting position and when the body is leaning to the right. Exhale the rest of the time.

Keep the head in line with the body and lean it slightly to the left to inhale.

One can, like in the standard cut, execute a closing or scissoring action with the legs at each arm movement, but it would be unnecessarily complicated and without much benefit to this style of swimming.

4th Style: Doggy paddle or standard cut with alternating leg movement.

The work of the arms is identical to that of the standard or Indian cuts, but without the hands' sculling action.

Arms are projected alternatively forward and slightly bent, elbows elevated highly and the cupped hands and brought along the body in a straight line by strongly pulling the water towards oneself.

The legs perform a standard breast stroke on the stomach motion, but they work in the opposite direction, instead of working symmetrically. While one leg does its return to the starting position, the other leg extends.

The simultaneous work of the upper and lower limbs occurs two ways:

- ◉ The left leg works at the same time as the right arm, and the left leg at the same time as the left arm;

- ◉ Or, the right leg works with the left arm and vice-versa.

Figure 22. Left: starting position for 1st effort. Right: end of 1st effort (left arm against the body, left leg extended laterally then brought back in line with the body) and starting position for 2nd effort. This style is done by working opposing limbs at the same time. This manner is easier as it is more natural.

The body remains constantly on the stomach during the swim.

The succession of the various phases of execution is the following, assuming the limbs of the same side work at the same time:

1st Phase: Starting position or preparation.

Arms position: right arm to the body, left arm out of the water, like in the standard or Indian cuts.

Legs position: left leg bent laterally, knee out, foot bent like in the breast stroke on the stomach. Right leg extended in the alignment of the body.

2nd Phase:1st impulse effort.

Bring the right arm in a straight line backwards by strongly pulling the water towards yourself and project the right arm forward, like in the standard or Indian cuts.

Extend the left leg and bring it in the alignment of the body; bend the right leg, knee out, as indicated in the breast stroke on the stomach.

3rd Phase: 2nd impulse effort.

Bring the right arm in a straight line backwards by strongly pulling the water towards yourself and project the left arm forward, like in the standard or Indian cuts.

Extend the right leg and bring it in the alignment of the body; bend the left leg, knee out, as indicated in the breast stroke on the stomach.

At the end of this 3rd phase the limbs find themselves in the starting position, ready to perform the 1st impulse effort again.

This swimming style goes on like so with a continuous series of equal and alternating impulse efforts. In this style, the effort from all the limbs is used for progression.

At no moment is the upper body unsupported or not raised to allow breathing to be performed easily and regularly. Inhales only occur at distant intervals after a few successive impulse efforts.

To inhale, it is necessary to provide a sufficient impulse with the hand to raise the head and upper body.

5th Style: Crawling swim or Indian cut with alternated leg movement.

This swimming style differs from the doggy paddle when it comes to the closing or "scissoring" of the legs, instead of taking place laterally like in the standard breast stroke, it takes place from front to back like in the Indian stroke or Indian cut. The knees are slightly spread apart front to back, but never lateral.

1st Phase: starting position or preparation.

Arms position: right arm alongside the body, left arm above the water like in the doggy paddle.

Legs position: Left hamstring slightly bent, left knee slight ahead of the right knee, left leg also bent, foot extended, heel as close to the hamstring as possible.

Right leg extended in the alignment of the body.

Figure 23. Left: starting position for 1st impulse. Right: end of 1st impulse, start of 2nd.

2nd Phase: 1st impulse effort.

Bring the left arm in a straight line backwards by strongly pulling the water to yourself and project the right arm forward, like in the doggy paddle. Vigorously extend the left leg and bring it in line with the body. Execute this movement as if giving a powerful kick with the entire anterior part of the leg. Before extending the leg, first bring the thigh back, the left leg slightly past the right knee.

Bend the right leg at the same time, as just described for the left leg.

3rd Phase: 2nd impulse effort.

Like the 2nd phase, but with actual work of the right arm and right leg.

Bring the right arm in a straight line backwards by strongly pulling the water towards you and project the right arm forward, as described in the 2nd phase.

Vigorously extend the right leg and bring it back in line with the body. At the same time, bend the left hamstring and leg, as just described for the right leg.

At the end of this 3rd phase, the limbs are in position to restart the 1st impulse effort. This swimming style goes on like this with a series of equal and alternated impulse efforts.

The movement of the legs, as it has just been described, can be compared quite similarly to an external form of the movement of the legs when riding a bicycle by retro-pedaling, meaning the opposite of standard bicycle pedaling.

Another manner to do this preceding leg movement exists, which gets rid of the return to the starting position and consequently any work impairing propulsion. It's the "double scissoring" movement. In the starting position, the legs are straight and spread, the left leg forward, the right leg back, feet extended.

During the 1st impulse effort, cross the legs and uncross them in the opposite direction, meaning bring the left leg back and right leg forward without bending the knees'.

During the 2nd impulse effort, cross and uncross the legs again.

At each effort, both legs work with equal force to provide the "double scissoring". When proceeding so the legs movement can be compared to, from an external form standpoint only, to the legs movement during marching/walking's leg extension.

Like in the doggy paddle, breathing is difficult in the crawl. Inhales only occur at distant intervals, after several successive impulse efforts.

The crawl, or crawling swim, allows to gain the fastest speed on very short distances.

IV. UNDERWATER DIVING/SWIMMING AND SWIMMING BETWEEN TWO WATERS.

"Diving" consists of immersing the body, as well as the head, under the surface of the water.

Swimming between two waters consists of, while diving, to cover a certain distance or reach a certain depth.

In this particular situation of the body in dive mode, it is obviously impossible to take in any air.

The duration of the immersion is, consequently, quite limited and its value depends on the more or lesser great tolerance of the cardiorespiratory function.

The "dive" is an exercise of capital importance. It is particularly useful when there is a need to:

- Cope when accidentally submerged;

- Handle agitated waters;

- Rescue someone who is either drowning or floating between two waters;

- Look for someone who fell in;

- Pick up an object from the bottom, etc.

The learning process of diving is done the following way:

- Step into shallow water, approximately to chest level;

- Take a long and deep inhale;

- At the end of the inhale, immediately submerge the entire head under water and hold on to that air intake in the chest as long as possible;

- Then, release air slowly with light exhales;

- As soon as the exhale is nearly complete and it is no longer possible to resist the urge for a new breath intake, emerge the head from the water;

◉ Repeat the same exercise several times successively, with a sufficient break between each trial.

Gradually train the body to stay without breathing for longer periods, either with the aforementioned method, or simply by submerging the head during the breast stroke on the stomach or during the upright swim.

Also train the eyes to remain widely *open* during the entirety of the dive.

Finally, get the ears used to bear the water pressure without discomfort.

Learn then to swim between two waters in the following fashion:

◉ Step into shallow water, about chest level. Take a long and deep inhale.

◉ Quickly squat down in order to submerge the entire body.

◉ Shoot forward by executing the movements of the breast stroke on the stomach or shoot backwards by executing the movements of the breast stroke on the back.

◉ Let the body return slowly to the surface by maintaining the head slightly higher than the feet.

Repeat this exercise in deep water.

While swimming upright, elevate the body above the surface as highly as possible with a vigorous impulse from the legs and the arms, while deeply inhaling at the same time.

Let the body sink vertically under the surface of the water, helping the motion if need be with an adequate hand movement.

Lower the upper body forward or backwards and shoot the body between two waters, as described before, by executing breast stroke movements either on the stomach or the back.

During the underwater dive, it might be necessary to:

1) Resurface frequently;

2) Sink deeper;

3) Remain between two waters;

4) Cover distance between two waters;

5) Remain still or "floating" between two waters.

Translator's note: the difference between 3 and 5 is simply a matter of motion: still versus treading water.

In order to resurface, straighten the upper body and position yourself vertically in order to perform the standard upright swim's movements. If the feet touch the bottom, push off with a powerful impulse.

In order to sink deeper, lower the upper body forward and perform opposite arm motions with the arms to that of the upright swim, meaning first lower the arms, palms vertical, then lift them up and bring them to the chest. As soon as the head is lower than the feet, strongly swim with the legs to shoot straight deeper, while continuing the same arm motion.

In order to remain between two waters, the body in any position: upright, on the stomach or on the back, maintain balance at a given depth with an adequate arm movement and an equally adequate hand position.

If the body tends to rise, pull the water towards you from bottom to top. If on the contrary the body tends to sink, push the water off with the hands from top to bottom.

Keep the legs still or move them once in a while, if needed, to help the descent or ascent of the body.

In order to cover distance between two waters, use the arms in an auxiliary fashion to help maintain balance at a given depth to prevent the body from sinking or rising. Progress both with the action of the legs and the arms.

In order to remain still or "floating" between two waters, the best way is to be on your stomach, the body folded in half, arms hanging naturally. In this position, a portion of the back or top of the skull is slightly emerged. It's in this position that many drowning victims are found, however.

The diving exercises always present a certain *risk*.

Follow an extremely slow progression as to the duration of the underwater "trips" or the depth reached[1]. At the first sensation of discomfort or unease, resurface as quickly as possible and get out of the water immediately.

(…)

[ORIGINAL TEXT MISSING AND PHOTO TOO BLURRY]

(…) of relative great depth, commands to have someone watching over you or better to be attached with a harness connected to a rope of sufficient length, whose extremity is handheld by a person standing on the bank.

Do not trust that just because you were able to dive for a certain amount of time on a given day that you could repeat that the next day or day after next without consequences. It all depends on the particular conditions you find yourself in. The body's tolerance is variable and any factor can influence it: digestion, nutrition, sleep, temperature, weather conditions, etc.

---

[1] This diving performance scale (duration) already shown in Chapter IX of the first part, in the scoring charts is the following:

10 seconds	0 points
20	1--------
30	2--------
40	3-------- (superior ability)
50	4--------
60	5-------- (exceptional ability)

etc.

By adopting the same grading process and same notation for all the scoring of the tests, the *depth* diving performance scale is the following:

3 meters/9.8 feet	0 points
4m/13.12ft	1--------
5m/16.4ft	2--------
6m/19.7ft	3-------- (superior ability)
7m/23ft	4--------
8m/26.2ft	5-------- (exceptional ability)

When dives of considerable *duration* are executed, it is prudent to not exceed depths of 3 to 4 meters (approximately 10 to 13 feet).

V. LAND DIVING HEAD OR FEET FIRST.

Diving head first or feet first from land consist of immersing oneself brutally.

This exercise is learned very quickly and without difficulty, as soon as one is capable of remaining in underwater dive and to swim between two waters. It is particularly useful if one wishes to:

1) Quickly jump into the water;

2) Instantly reach a great depth;

3) Not be surprised in case of an accidental fall;

4) Quickly shoot in any given direction;

5) Quickly catch someone in danger of drowning;

Etc.

Learning how to dive begins by *jumping in the water, feet first.*

Figure 24. Jump into the water like for a broad and depth jump. Or: jump in a squatted position, trunk nearly vertical, by grabbing hold of the shins and pointing the toes before entering the water. Or: jump upright, body fully extended, arms alongside the body, extended laterally or vertically.

Stand at the edge of the water, feet level with it or slightly higher than surface level.

Take a deep breath in, then jump in the water for a true broad and depth jump.

While suspended in mid-air, *maintain the body in balance* and slightly bend the lower limbs as if the landing were on solid ground, represented by the water's surface. Instead of spreading the knees for the landing, tightly squeeze them in order to protect the genitals from the impact on the water.

Let the arms hang loosely, or, if desired, to reduce the sinking depth of the body, extend them horizontally, hands flat upon entry into the water.

The body, once fully immersed, finds itself in an underwater dive. Proceed as explained previously to rise back up to the surface or to progress between two waters.

Repeat this exercise by jumping from a higher level, little by little.

In order to dive from a very high spot, feet first, squat down completely, knees together and close to the chest, head lowered, chin on chest, hands holding on to the front of the legs.

By proceeding so, the body is balled up and, regardless of the height of the jump; no dangerous shock or impact is to be feared upon arrival in the water.

It is also possible to jump in the water feet first, by keeping the body stiff, legs together and completely extended and the arms glued to the body, upon arrival in the water. However, this manner is far less practical than the previous.

Diving head first is done the following way:

Stand at the edge of the water, feet level with it or slightly higher than surface level.

Take a deep breath in, preparing for a true broad and depth jump.

Execute the following sequence of moves:

Figure 25.1) Inhale deeply and raise the arms. 2) Lower the arms and bring them back while bending the legs, upper body leaning forward. 3) Extend the limbs vigorously by projecting the arms quickly above the head.

Raise the arms straight forward, then lower them down and back while bending the legs.

At the same time, lower the upper body and at the precise moment where it will tip forward, vigorously extend the legs by powerfully projecting the arms beyond the head, in alignment with the trunk (impulse).

Figure 26. 2nd subject from left, about to fall forward, must extend the legs and bring arms over the head. Subject on far right left the bank, lower limbs fully extended, arms extended past the head. The body enters at an angle of roughly 45º. Chin is tucked on the chest shortly before entering the water.

As soon as the feet leave the ground, fully extend the lower limbs, knees and heels joined, toes pointed.

Join the thumbs of each hand above the head, palms down and flat, arms straight.

While suspended in mid-air, the arms, the trunk and the legs are fully extended and in the same alignment.

Enter the water with the head at an angle of about 45°, taking advantage of the impulse given by the legs. The hands and arms need to carve a path for the head, which must absorb the impact of the water precisely on the *top of the skull* and not on the forehead or face.

Repeat the same exercise by increasing the elevation of the jump.

Figure 27. A proper dive produces no splash, the body penetrates the water like an arrow. The direction of the body's speed must be precisely in line with the body itself at the moment the body enters the water.

The higher the elevation, the less powerful the impulse given by the legs needs to be.

Note that diving head first, just like diving feet first, is a *true jump*. Upon landing in the water, the body must be completely extended and powered by a certain amount of speed in the direction of the line it is forming.

Figure 28. Example of a high dive head first. The higher the elevation, the less powerful the impulse from the legs. Do not enter the water too vertically, to avoid too deep an entry. "Glide" as long as possible by maintaining the head higher than the feet. Only lower the upper body 1 or 2 meters (3 to 6 feet) before the water surface.

The most common errors in the manner of executing this exercise consists of:

1) *Not giving enough impulse with the legs.* The body then falls vertically in the water like a dead object instead of entering at an angle like an arrow. The impact of the water on the stomach, the chest or the face can be very painful.

2) *Not straightening the legs while in suspension in mid-air or spreading them and bending them under the basin.* This way produces big splashes and a violent shock on the hamstrings. A correct dive produces no splashing.

3) *Not letting the body tilt forward enough,* which causes a painful landing on the stomach and the face.

4) *Tilting forward too much,* which causes either a painful landing on the back, or a complete somersault of the body once in the water.

Figure 29. Another high dive example of a head first dive, with an adjustable level diving board.

It is important to distinguish:

1) A dive to instantly reach a great depth;

2) A dive to shoot as quickly as possible in any given direction;

In order to achieve a great depth instantly, tilt the upper body in such a way as to enter the water nearly vertically.

In order to shoot as far as possible in any direction, enter the water, by contrast, at an angle below 45º in order to sink under the surface as little as possible, between 50cm and 1m of depth (1.5 to 3 feet).

Just before arriving to the surface of the water, while still suspended in mid-air, give a strong "hold" of the head and chest backwards in order to "cut" the water at a low angle.

Arch the back well at the same time to avoid a belly flop.

As soon as in the water, instantly start swimming and let the head emerge naturally.

This style of diving by taking in as little water as possible requires a relatively long practice to be executed perfectly, meaning the head emerging before even the feet get immersed beneath the surface. It is particularly useful to immerse in waters whose depth is unknown.

Diving from land, just like underwater diving, presents always a certain danger.[2]

In some cases, *the shock of the water* on the face produces the effect of a strong slap, or the reached depth being too great can produce a dazing effect capable of preventing a return to the surface.

Belly-flops, flat-back landings or hamstring slaps resulting from execution mistakes by spearing the head produce a whiplash effect, and are therefore quite painful, especially when only basic swim trunks are worn. Everything that was mentioned relative to the dangers of underwater diving generally applies to land dives, head or feet first.

It is cautioned to watch out for those wishing to achieve greater depths, dive from a high elevation or remain underwater for a while without resurfacing, or even to attach them to a harness with a long enough rope.

Before spearing the head, beginners must always ensure that the water is deep enough and is at least 3 meters (10 feet) deep.

---

[2] By adopting the same process of scoring and recording of all the events listed in Chapter IX of the 1st part, the scale of land dive performances, *head first,* can be the following:

From surface level _____	0 points	
1m (3') above surface _____	1---------	
2m (6.5') _____	2----------	
3m (10') _____	3---------	(superior ability)
4m (13') _____	4 --------	
5m (16.5') _____	5---------	(exceptional ability)

VI. RESCUE EXERCISES

Swimming using only arms or legs. – Diving with all manners possible. – Carrying objects. – Picking up objects. – Provide rescue. –Assist a rescuer in trouble. –Rescue of a sunken or capsized boat. –Crossing a stream and establishing a back-and-forth action. –Clothed swimming.

From a functional standpoint, swimming exercises have to have as essential goal training on and under water, without which no rescue training is possible.

The following exercises are chosen and classified in a way that allows to progressively prepare the swimmer to manage any situation and also to rescue a person in danger of drowning.

They must be executed first in proper swimming apparel before thinking to do them clothed.

I. SWIMMING WITH THE ARMS OR LEGS ONLY.

1) Swim on the stomach, on the back, upright and sideways with both legs and only one arm.

   Immobilize the other arm by placing the hand at the hip, behind the neck, overhead, etc. *(Translator's note: refer to the second part, Fundamental Exercises, Chapter III).*

2) Swim on the stomach, back, upright or sideways with only the legs. Immobilize the arms by placing the hands at the hips, behind the neck, above the head etc.

3) Swim on the stomach, back, upright or sideways with the arms only. Maintain the legs together and extended, in line with the body.

4) Progress with one arm only, the other limbs still, in any position.

5) Progress with one leg only, the other limbs still, in any position.

II. LAND DIVE IN ANY MANNER POSSIBLE.

1) Dive feet first and come back to the surface of the water as quickly as possible by facing the same direction as at the start.

2) Spear the dive head first and immediately resurface in the same direction as the start by remaining as shallow water as possible.

3) Spear a head first dive at any possible angle.

4) Dive feet first and resurface as quickly as possible facing the starting point. To do that, do a half-turn in the water before resurfacing.

5) Dive head first and resurface as quickly as possible facing the starting point. To do that, do a half-turn in the water before resurfacing.

6) Dive with momentum, feet first. Do a preliminary run and look to jump with momentum as far and as deeply as possible.

Figure 31. Clothed swimmers carrying a rifle, holding it at the shoulder with one arm.

7) Dive head first with momentum. Start with a preliminary run, followed by a push-off with both feet and project yourself head first as far as possible.

   Repeat the same exercise without the two-legged push-off.

8) Dive head first with or without momentum and resurface facing the starting position after having performed a complete somersault/flip in the water.

9) Fall backwards in any way possible: return to the surface forward and on the stomach, or facing backwards and on the back.

   Never fully extend the body while falling; *on the contrary bend the trunk* as much as possible towards the legs once suspended in mid-air and strongly bring the head to the chest to avoid a painful flat fall on the back.

10) Fall in the water "by surprise" by getting pushed by somebody.

III. CARRY OBJECTS MORE OR LESS BUOYANT THAN THE WATER.

1) Remain on the surface of the water by holding on to any object: buoy, oar, board, piece of driftwood, etc.

   Maintain the object under the armpit or place the arms on it.

2) Push or pull a floating object in the water. Swim on the stomach, the back or the side, according to the shape of the object.

3) Carry a light object, which cannot get wet. Hold it by hand above the water, the arm bent, or maintain it on the head with one or both arms.

Figure 32.Carrying objects heavier than water. Swimmers crossing a river with rifles.

4) Carry a heavier than water object from one spot to the next.

Figure 33. Example of carrying clothes without getting them wet.

Maintain the object on the shoulder, the head or attach it to the back or the belt.

In the case where the object is attached to the body, it is prudent to watch out for the swimmer or to attach him with a belt or harness connected to a sufficiently long rope.

5) Carry clothes without getting them wet.

   For that, make a tight package, solidly sealed. Place it on the head, slowly enter the water and swim upright maintaining it with one or both hands.

IV. PICK UP OBJECTS BY DIVING UNDERWATER.

1) Start by diving at depths of 2 meters to start (about 6.5 feet), in very clear water, and pick up very light and visible objects such as: pebbles, white stones, plates, bottles, etc.

   Perform the exercise by diving using all manners possible, head or feet first.

Figure 34. Picking up objects by diving underwater.

Gradually increase the depth of the water and weight of the objects.

Train to also pick up objects in agitated waters.

2) Catch falling objects and sinking between two waters. For that, quickly spear the dive head first slightly below where the object fell in and look to catch it during its descent.

3) Perform the preceding exercise, being already in the water at the moment the object falls in. Rise up above the water with a vigorous impulse from the legs and immediately let yourself sink below the surface, feet first, lower then the body to swim between two waters. Never bend or lower the body to dive deeply before being fully under the surface; otherwise, the legs emerge and slow down the descent.

4) Dive with a rope and attach it to an object at the bottom. This exercise is useful to retrieve objects too heavy to be brought back to the surface by only holding them with the hands.

V. PROVIDE RESCUE.

There are several cases to consider:

1) *The person in need of rescuing is not in danger doesn't require immediate help* and still possess a portion of its abilities. The person is simply exhausted or doesn't have the strength to reach a landing spot.

2) *The person to rescue has no strength left* and is incapable of any movement as a result of cramping or stiffness in all their limbs. If the person doesn't know how to float, he or she is in danger of sinking.

Figure 35. Helping someone not in immediate danger: the person needing rescue places their hands on the rescuer, gets towed from the back or the side.

3) *The person in need of rescue is flailing desperately* and seeks to hang on to the rescuer by any means necessary.

Based on the circumstances, use, to simply help or to actually rescue, one of the following indicated means.

In preparation for the role of the rescuer, execute the various exercises between two waters, which alternatively fulfill the roles of rescuer and rescued.

In the rescue drills, the rescuer must attempt all efforts to keep the person to rescue's head above water *at all times*.

The rescuer can, if needed, inhale at irregular intervals and doesn't hesitate to keep their head underwater and stay immersed for a few seconds, when necessary.

The rescue drills can also be done with a special dummy, resembling an ordinary person in shape and dimension.

The dummy should be weighted at will, so that it can float at the surface, remain between two waters or directly sink, according to the desired exercise to practice.

1st Manner: *Help the person in need of rescuing by having the person place one or both hands on the shoulder(s) of the rescuer.*

Figure 36. No immediate danger: the person to rescue puts their hands on the rescuer's shoulders. The rescuer thus maintains or tows the person in need by facing them and swimming on their stomach or better, their back.

The rescuer approaches the person that needs rescue from the front, side or back. The person maintains contact with the rescuer or lets them tow them one of two ways:

1) By simply placing one hand on the rescuer's shoulder.

2) By placing both hands on the rescuer's shoulders, either from the front, or the back of the rescuer.

The person needing rescue remains still on the stomach or on the back, legs extended, or swims using the free arm and the legs if they have enough strength for it.

The rescuer tows the person on the stomach or the back and also swims on the stomach or back, depending on the case.

Figure 37. Seize the victim from behind with both hands, above the elbows or under the armpits. Tow the person by swimming using the legs only, preferably on the back.

This method of providing help, especially with one hand, is quite practical to cover long distances; it also allows strong swimmers to aid weaker ones to traverse a stream, for instance.

This needs to be taught right away to beginners in order to give reassurance to those watching them or accompanying them.

2nd Manner: The rescuer grabs the victim with a single hand.

The rescuer approaches the victim from the front, the side or the back and immediately places a hand under the armpit or grabs the arm above the elbow.

Figure 38. Grabbing hold from the back, either under the armpits or the arms, is the safest and most practical. It prevents the rescuer from being grabbed.

3rd Manner: *The rescuer grabs the victim with both hands.*

Figure 39. Person in need (left) is grabbed frontally with both hands, either by the arms above the elbows, or under the armpits. Tow the person by swimming with the legs only, preferably on the back.

The rescuer approaches the victim from behind and grabs them with both hands, either by the arms above the elbows, under the armpits or both sides of the neck. The rescuer then swims using the legs only, on the stomach or preferably the back.

This manner is the most practical ad the safest to rescue a person who lost all their abilities.

4th Manner: *Grab the person and hug them with a single arm.*

The rescuer approaches the person to save from behind. He or she grabs the left arm, for instance, under the left armpit or above the left shoulder in order to wrap the arm around the neck or chest.

He/she then swims on the back or side with both legs and one arm.

If the victim is clothed, the left hand can find a hold in the clothes.

Figure 40. Grab victim from behind with both hands, hooked into the clothes on both sides of the neck or upper chest. Tow swimming backwards, with legs only. The rescuer may have to sacrifice their own breathing at times to keep the victim's head above water.

This manner is as practical and as safe as the previous; moreover, it allows to move along more quickly.

Figure 41. Grab the victim frmo behind by surrounding the neck with the left arm and hooking into the clothes with the left hand. Swim on the back or the side with both hands and one arm.

Figure 42 a & b: rescue from behind using one arm only. This method makes things easier for the rescuer and allows him to swim quickly and easily on his back or side with both legs and one arm.

5th Manner: *2-rescuers at once for one victim.*

Figure 43. The rescuers are positioned one in front, one in back, and grab the victim by the arms or under the armpits. They keep his head above water, swimming upright with the legs only.

Both rescuers approach the victim, one from the front, one from behind, or one on each side. They keep the person afloat using one of the aforementioned methods, meaning by grabbing the victim under the armpits or by the arms.

The victim can also, if capable, place both hands on the rescuers.

6ᵗʰ Manner: *2-rescuer transport of one victim.*

Figure 44. Rescuers are in front and back, grabbing the victim by armpits or arms. One swims on his back, the other on his stomach so as to keep the victim on the back during towing. That way, the head stays above water.

Figure 45. Rescuers positions themselves on both sides of the victim, hooking one arm in his clothes. In that position, both swim on their stomach to keep the person on his back while towing.

Approach and grab the victim as just described and swim by towing.

If the rescuers are split one in the front, one in the back, one of them swims on the back, the other on the stomach. The victim is consequently either on their stomach or back as well, depending on the case.

If both rescuers are positioned at each side, they swim on the stomach, the back or the side, by towing the victim either on the stomach, or preferably on the back.

VI. ASSIST A RESCUER IN TROUBLE.

In order to avoid being undertaken by a victim that is frantic in the water, *always approach the victim from behind* and immediately grab the person under the armpits or by the arms above the elbows. Hold on tightly. If the person tries to turn around to grab the rescuer, the latter ought to, instead of resisting, also turn at the same time in order to remain behind the victim's back.

The rescuer can be grabbed by the victim in various ways:

1) By the wrists;

2) By the arms;

3) By the neck;

4) With a bear hug;

Figure 46. Left group: rescuer (left) grabbed bu the wrists, turns them inside and extendes his arms laterally. Right group: rescuer (right) grabbed at the waist and one arm, gets away with a wrestling parry of a frontal belt.

5) By the legs;

6) From behind;

7) By the clothes.

As a general rule, to rapidly get away and avoid getting caught too close, use some *self-defense parries*, in particular the frontal belt, which consists of pushing off the opponent with the forearm placed on the throat or neck.

If the victim has a stronghold, use one of the following ways to get away:

1) *If grabbed by the wrists*, turn the wrists internally by powerfully extending the arms laterally.

2) *If grabbed by the neck*, position, for instance, the left hand behind the victim's back and the right hand over their arms and on their chin. Then, strongly push off the victim's head backwards

Figure 47. Left group: rescuer (left) grabbed at the neck, places the left hand behind the victim's neck and pushes back hard with the right hand against the head, backwards. Right group: rescuer (right), grabbed at the waist, gets away by pushing the head back applying a knee to the stomach.

3) *If grabbed by the arms,* from the front, the stomach or by one arm on the side, swim upright, the stomach or back using the legs only. This type of hold presents no danger to the rescuer.

4) *If grabbed with a hear hug,* place the right hand on the victim's chin or the forearm across their throat. At the same time, place the left hand on their right shoulder and push hard with the knee or either foot on the victim's stomach. Quickly push the person away backwards, with the hands and either knee or foot that serves as anchor point.

Figure 48. Rescuer places the left hand under the chin and pushes the head back to make them lose their hold.

5) *If grabbed by the legs,* swim using the arms to remain on the surface. The victim having their head under water will inevitably choke or lose consciousness; as a result, they won't be able to maintain the hold for long.

   In all cases, there is nothing to fear from this type of hold, regardless of the victim's weight, as it is always possible to remain afloat using the arms only.

6) *If grabbed from behind,* immediately position yourself on the back and strongly maintain that position by swimming with the legs. Either way, the rescuer has nothing to fear, because the victim has their head under water and will quickly run out of air, or their head is above water and the rescue proceeds smoothly.

7) *To release a hold on clothing,* grab one or several fingers of the victim and twist them vigorously.

VII. RESCUE OF A SUNKEN OR CAPSIZED BOAT.

Embark several swimmers onto a light boat rid of all non-floating objects. Begin to progressively sway the boat from side to side, in order to fill it then capsize it.

At the moment it capsizes, the boaters *flee and move away as quickly as possible*. Then, they immediately return and regroup *at the front and the back* and make all out efforts to reposition it back to normal.

Figure 49. Capsized boat. As the boat is capsizing, the passengers escape and get away from it as quickly as possible, in order to not remain caught under with it's upside down.

They divide on each side, in about equal numbers, and place their hands on the washboards in order to keep the boat straight. In that position, they wait for rescue by holding on to the washboards, or tow the boat by swimming in order to land at any spot.

If a bucket or bowl is available, and if the boat is floating so its washboards are above the surface level, one of the boaters can climb aboard to dump water off the boat. As the water in the boat reduces, the boaters can successively climb aboard.

Be careful, when a boat sinks then capsizes, *to get rid of objects that can tangle the limbs as quickly as possible,* especially the legs, to swim away/flee quickly, in order to not be under the boat when it's upside down.

Figure 50. As the boat is capsizing, quickly get rid of any objects susceptible of entangling limbs, legs especially.

Figure 51. Once capsized, get back to the boat and attempt to right it.

Performing the following exercise:

Let the boat fill up by loading with an excessive number of boaters, or by causing light side-to-side sways, or by removing the plug-hole.

As the boat sinks, the boaters try to maintain it upright in order to prevent its capsizing. They empty it afterwards and make it float again without having had it capsize.

To jettison some weight quickly, some of the boaters may jump off the boat if necessary.

Figure 52. The sunken and capsized boat is maintained upright by the swimmers, spread out on each side. In this situation, they await rescue or swim and tow it.

Note: these exercises presenting a certain dangers, it is prudent at the beginning to anchor the boaters and to have the anchors held by helpers on land or in a nearby boat.

VIII. CROSSING A STREAM AND ESTABLISHING A BACK-AND-FORTH ACTION.

To cross a stream wearing clothes or any kind of object, mainly when the pathway is considerable and the current very strong, proceed the following way:

Makeshift a light raft, a basic frame if need be, with branches, boards, beams etc., tied together with ropes or pieces of ripped cloth. Lay the objects to transport on it.

Figure 53. A simple raft is the most practical and safest means to cover some ground or cross a river with poor swimmers or people not able to swim at all. In the latter case, the individuals tie themselves strongly to the raft.

Tow the makeshift raft by pushing or pulling as mentioned for objects that can float. Rest on the way if need be, using the raft as support.

When no boat is available, a basic raft is the safest and most practical way to cross a river with de-conditioned individuals or not capable of swimming. If the raft is sufficiently solid, the people who can't swim can be on it. In the opposite situation, they can simply find support on the sides of the raft. They can also strongly attach themselves to the raft itself, if they fear not having enough strength to hold on for the duration of the course. Others who can swim may also hang on to the raft and can tow it by pushing or pulling it.

For added safety, all the swimmers can tie ropes to the raft itself.

When the number of people is too large to find a spot around the raft or on the raft, it is of course necessary to make several trips and the best swimmers must in that case bring the raft to its starting point.

If a rope of sufficient length is available, a back-and-forth movement is established between the two banks.

At the raft's first trip, one end of the rope is taken, while the other stays with the people left on the bank. The ends of the back-and-forth are then solidly attached on each bank and the tight rope serves as a towing means for the swimmers who bring the raft.

Instead of affixing both ends of the back-and-forth action on the banks, the ends can be attached to the raft itself.

The individuals who have not crossed yet easily bring the raft to them, after the first group disembarked. If the ropes are long enough, a back-and-forth action can be established on both banks.

The raft then crosses in both directions, without the need for swimmers to tow it. When crossing a river, *never fight the current;* always land at a spot downstream from the starting point.

IX. CLOTHED SWIMMING.

Begin with only wearing a pair of boxers and some shoes. Gradually add-on more articles of clothing until fully clothed. Repeat the following exercises, especially work above water and underwater, while fully clothed.

Swimming when clothed is *extremely tiring* and also quite slow.

First of all, *floatability is lesser* than when in swim trunks, except for a short duration of time, immediately after immersion, when the water hasn't fully soaked the clothes. This reduction in floatability often renders the exercise of floating without moving impossible.

Moreover, the limbs cannot have a full range of motion, because of the inconvenience caused by the clothes.

Finally, the pockets of water formed by the clothes provide a considerable obstacle to propulsion.

Generally, the rhythm of the swimming motions while clothed must be slower than that of swimming in proper swim apparel to avoid unnecessary fatigue.

While fully clothed in the water, it is *possible to completely undress.* This exercise is at once an application of the upright swim, of "floating", of underwater diving and swimming with the arms or legs only.

The removal of the cardigan and vest is the only portion of the drill that's relatively easy. One needs to only maintain a vertical stance by swimming upright using the legs only.

To take off shoes, pants and underwear, it is necessary to squat and remain underwater for a few moments to take off each article of clothing.

To remove the shirt or undershirt, swim upright and go under if necessary in order to take them off more easily over the head.

Aside from the cardigan and vest, the removal of the pants, shirt and shoes is both annoying and tiring, even at times exhausting.

Plus, the pants and underwear can stay stuck and thus reduce the usage of the legs.

The shirt and undershirt can also stay stuck on the head and cause submersion.

To sum up, if it is necessary to remove a few articles of clothing, *it can be dangerous to undress fully in the event of accidental submersion.*

VII. ACCIDENTAL SUBMERSION

Getting out of danger when accidentally submerged. - Rescue someone in danger. – First aid to drowning victims.

I. GETTING OUT OF DANGER IN CASE OF ACCIDENTAL SUBMERSION.

After an accidental fall, resurface as quickly as possible the catch your breath.

Maintain calm to judge the situation, think of managing your strength and especially do no unnecessary movements. If a rescue spot is nearby, reach it as quickly as possible fully clothed. If it is far, swim with great precaution and pace yourself to avoid fatigue.

Get rid, if need be, of the easiest articles of clothing to remove, like a cardigan or vest.

There may be times when keeping the vest is of interest to prevent pockets from filling in the shirt.

In any case, unless one is of exceptional strength, *never attempt to fully undress.*

It is better to keep all your clothes than to expose yourself to fatigue or exhaustion by wanting to get rid of them.

If the current is too strong, do not waste strength in fighting it, seek to land downstream from the present position or await rescue.

To get away from a whirlpool or from the grasp of aquatic vegetation, do not resist, on the contrary remain still and passive by floating for a little while.

II. RESCUE SOMEONE IN DANGER.

The first duty of the rescuer is to act with *extreme speed,* as any wasted moment can have fatal consequences.

Rescue is relatively easy if the person to rescue is still only just endangered. Get close and grab hold of them by using any of the previously described means, then await rescue or swim towards a favorable spot.

In all circumstances, the safest and most practical means consists of approaching the person *from behind* and grab them by the arms or under the armpits before they realize it. That way, the rescuer is not apprehended by the victim.

In the event that the victim manages to turn around and grab the rescuer, the latter escapes immediately and returns once again from behind a few moments later.

If the rescuer has been grabbed, he will employ one of the means described previously under the heading **"VI. Assist a rescuer in trouble".** As an extreme measure, if the situation is even too perilous for the rescuer, no hesitation is to occur to suffocate or make the victim lose consciousness.

Rescue becomes more difficult when the person, having sunken straight to the bottom, doesn't resurface.

If the rescuer saw the person disappear, he must guide himself in his search with the help of the *air bubbles*, which indicate the exact submersion spot. He dives before or after those bubbles according to the current's direction. If there is no precise indicator of the disappearance spot, he explores the bottom through successive dives.

The rescuer has nothing to fear when it comes to being grabbed by a fully submerged individual. So long as the latter doesn't resurface, meaning that they've lost consciousness or worse, it means they do not have any strength left.

When one is caught fully clothed when having to perform a rescue, do not waste precious time undressing fully, especially if the distance to cover is minimal.

Only get rid of the most encumbering objects: cardigan and shoes.

Adjust the pants at the waist, in order to avoid having the legs immobilized.

III. FIRST AID TO DROWNING VICTIMS.

As soon as the drowning victim is out of the water, perform in sequence the following actions:

1) Lay the victim flat on their back or a bit on their side, horizontally or with the head slightly higher than the feet;

2) Quickly loosen the clothes at the chest and waist;

3) Rid the mouth and nose of mucus. Maintain the mouth open, by introducing, if need be, between the teeth, any object such as a knife's handle, a stick of wood, a cork, etc.

4) Kneel behind the victim's head, grab their wrists and make them artificially perform *respiratory movements*.

For that, strongly press the wrists against the lower ribs, then pull them towards yourself above the head, in order to extend the arms in the line of the trunk, either straight or laterally.

Figure 54. Artificial Breathing (CPR equivalent then): Strongly press the victims' wrists on the lower ribs, then pull them towards you to bring the straight arms under the head in the alignment of the trunk.

Perform artificial breathing movements at the usual cadence of ordinary breathing, meaning 15 to 20 per minute, which corresponds on average to 2 seconds for raising, 2 seconds for lowering.

The most practical means of observing this cadence is to *calibrate to yourself,* meaning to match the raising and the lowering with one's own inhales and exhales.

5) If after 4 or 5 minutes, breathing hasn't returned, cease the raising and lowering of the arms and replace them with *pulling of the tongue*.

   For that, grab the victim's tongue with a handkerchief, a piece of cloth, etc., pull it towards you relatively energetically, then let it return naturally.

   Pulling needs to be done like the arm movements, at the *same cadence as ordinary breathing movements*, meaning 15 to 20 times per minute.

6) As soon as breathing returns, undress the victim fully, rub them with dry towels, blankets or simply dry clothes, in order to reanimate.

Then, cover or dress with dry clothes and carry the person if need be.

Figure 55. 1st rescuer does breathing movements with the arms, 2nd performs the rhythmic pulling of the tongue, 3rd rubs the drowning victim with a dry towel or piece of clothing. The elevation movement of the arms must match the tongue pulls.

7) Never stop too soon, or despair giving aid to a drowning victim. Continue artificial respiration and tongue pulls as long as possible; even for hours in some cases.

   What has been just described only applies in the case of a single person with a drowning victim. If several individuals are around, the most experienced among them but take the lead on the actions to perform.

   Four people at the most are necessary for urgent care; a greater number would mutually interfere with one another.

   One person takes care of undressing the victim;

A second person does the artificial respiration movements with the arms;

A third does the rhythmic tongue pulls;

Finally, a fourth person can assist the first in undressing and warming up the victim.

The second and third must match their actions from a rhythmic standpoint and pay attention that *the raising of the arms coincides exactly with the pulling of the tongue out.*

The care described here for drowning victims also applies to choking victims.

VIII. PROGRAMMING AND PRECAUTIONS RELATING TO GROUP INSTRUCTION OF SWIMMING EXERCISES.

Swimming must become a *regular exercise activity,* under the same rules as all other training, and not just free wading.

For group instruction to follow its due course, it is necessary that the students unable to swim must be learn to maintain themselves at the surface as soon as possible.

Begin by demonstrating, then properly executing "on dry land" the movements of the regular breast stroke on the stomach and back to all students who do not know how to swim.

When these movements are perfectly understood and performed, a maximum of 3 to 4 sessions, with a capable coach or instructor, always suffice for a student to be able to maintain themselves at the water's surface.

Figure 56. Swimming group instruction: beginning of a complete session: sudden immersion head or feet first.

Students already knowing how to swim well assist the masters for the initial instruction of the unskilled swimmers.

This instruction is done either along the bank holding the student anchored by a belt or rope, or by simply holding the student's hand when the depth allows a foothold.

The daily training program depends both on the weather conditions and the various abilities of the students. In general, a group training session always contains the successive execution of the following exercises:

1) Diving from land either head or feet first;

2) Diving underwater;

3) Group exercises with a progressive course in which various swimming styles are applied;

4) One or more additional specialized exercises according to the master's instructions;

5) A final speed swim.

The group exercises are very entertaining, and also, very useful for developing the swimmer's *self-confidence and agility.*

For their execution, the master instructors make the students adopt the various formations, of which the main ones are:

◉ Column (squad file);

◉ Row (squad rank);

◉ Swimming circle.

Figure 57. Group swim instruction: Separate groups. Swimmers are paired up with a strong swimmer and a weaker one.

They go from one formation to the next, thus performing a half-turn, facing right, left, or swimming on the stomach, or the back, or upright.

Figure 58. Group swim instruction: full platoon of marines by training group. The marines are fully clothed, first two groups carry a rifle in bandoleer. On the bank, in swim apparel, the master swimmers are ready for any rescue.

In order to get the students accustomed to swimming with the legs only to assist one another, the master instructors order these additional drills:

1) *Squad file on the stomach*

and *on the back*

(each student placing their hands on the hips, shoulders or under the armpits of the one before them).

2) *Squad rank* on the stomach or the back, each student placing a hand on their neighbor's shoulder.

During the training in the water, the students must always be "partnered up" in doubles, a strong swimmer with a weaker one.

Figure 59. End of complete session with a short distance speed swim.

Regardless of the type of drill, these two students always find themselves next to one another, thus increasing safety precautions.

Swims are done before meals or at least three hours after.

The most minute dispositions, but also the most practical are always taken prior to swimming in order to ensure a rapid rescue if need be.

A sufficient number of lifeguards equipped with lifesavers, ropes, poles etc., are always positioned in appropriate spots.

[INSERT PICS GALORE]

Some of the stronger swimmers are in swim apparel and attached with a belt whose end is always held by another swimmer or solidly anchored.

They must always keep their eyes on the students and always *be ready to assist* in any potential risk. Their preferred position is on the banks or in rescue boats.

For the duration of the swimming exercises, *the utmost silence and order* must be strictly observed. The voices of the master instructors and other coaches must be the only ones heard. It is the only way to prevent irreparable accidents, which can happen nearly instantly.

IX. PERFORMANCE CHARACTERIZING THE INDIVUAL "CAPABLE OF SWIMMING" AND THE "MASTER SWIMMER"[3]

To be considered "capable", an individual must be able to execute the following minimum requirements:

1) A 100-meter course in 3 minutes (or at the very least without a time limit);

2) An underwater dive of 10 seconds, the body fully submerged;

These performances match up to a "0" on the test scale of swimming drills contained in the scorecard.

A "master swimmer" is an individual knowledgeable not only in the various swimming processes, but also possessing the physical abilities to perform a difficult rescue.

The master swimmer must above all be an excellent diver. This quality is indeed indispensable:

◉ To search for someone between two waters in danger of drowning;

◉ To keep the rescued person's head above the water by sacrificing their own breathing if needed;

Other qualities the master swimmer must have are: speed, resistance to fatigue and cold, boldness to jump in the water, ease of movement and assessment between waters, agility to grab hold and tow a person in danger and finally, competency to care for drowning victims.

The diving ability required of a master swimmer cannot be under 60 seconds to have someone you can count on in case of dangers. Such a performance proves, indeed, excellent conditioning of internal organs like the lungs and the heart, and a great tolerance of the cardiovascular and respiratory functions.

---

[3] These performances, established after numerous experiments at the Navy infantry school, became regulatory in the Navy. By the Secretary/Minister's order of April 4, 1907, a certificate of "master swimmer" was awarded to any sailor having satisfied all the requirements.

It provides the certainty that the subject having achieved that at least once would be able to, at any time, even if not having exercised or swam for a long time, repeated dives of 15 to 30 seconds, on average, which is enough in practicality.

This 60-second performance ought to be achieved only after a few weeks' worth of conditioning. It can obviously only be delivered by individuals constantly training.

Individuals who train to become master swimmers must undergo a full medical exam comprising a careful examination of the lungs, heart and ears.

One or more master swimmers must be on deck for group swimming exercises.

The abilities required of a master swimmer are the following (with a water temperature assumed at 17° or 18° Celsius, 62°-65° Fahrenheit):

1) Speed test; 100 meters in 2 minutes.

2) Endurance test: 1000 meters (1 Kilometer) in 30 minutes[4].

3) Dive head first from a height of 5 meters (15ft).[5]

4) Remain 60 seconds underwater, body fully submerged.

5) Fully clothed (full "city dress" suit), pick up an object 3 meters deep (10ft), weighing about 5kg (11lb.)[6]

6) Fully clothed (as above), execute, with a dummy or a live volunteer, a "rescue" of a person in risk of drowning and cover a distance of 25 meters (82ft).

7) Justify through theoretical and practical knowledge how to administer care to drowning victims.

---

[4] By adopting the same process of grading and the same scoring in Chapter IX of the first Part/Book, the performance scale of the 1000 meter course is the following:

30 minutes_____0 points
29 _____1_____
28 _____2_____
27 _____3_____
26 _____4_____
25 _____5_____
etc.

[5] In shallow water preferably, about 3 meters deep (10ft).
[6] In relatively calm water, preferably.